You Were Born for More

A Journey of Faith, Mentorship, and Purpose

Author – Eld Joel Latimore Jr.

You Were Born for More

A Journey of Faith, Mentorship, and Purpose

Written by Eld Joel Latimore Jr.

© 2025 Eld Joel Latimore Jr.

ISBN (paperback): 979-8-218-83375-6

Latimore Publishing

All rights reserved.

No part of this book may be reproduced, stored in a retrieval system, or transmitted in any form or by any means—electronic, mechanical, photocopying, recording, or otherwise—without the prior written permission of the publisher, except for brief quotations used in reviews or scholarly works.

Scripture quotations are taken from the King James Version (KJV) of the Bible, unless otherwise noted.

Table of Contents

- Dedication

- Preface

- Mission Statement

- Introduction   **Pg 1**

- Why Black Youth Need…   **Pg 19**

Chapter 1 – The Crisis of Lost Identity   **Pg 35**

Chapter 2 – The Power of Guidance…   **Pg 54**

Chapter 3 – Learning to Follow…   **Pg 76**

Chapter 4 – When God Develops You…   **Pg 91**

Chapter 5 – Positioned for Purpose   **Pg 110**

Chapter 6 – Mentored by the Mission… **Pg 127**

Chapter 7 – Staying the Course   **Pg 147**

Chapter 8 – From Mentee to Mentor…   **Pg 167**

Chapter 9 – Passing the Baton…   **Pg 190**

Chapter 10: The Mentor's Reward…   **Pg 217**

Chapter 11 – The Mantle and the …	**Pg 240**
Closing Word	**Pg 264**
Acknowledgments	**Pg 268**
About the Author	**Pg 271**

Dedication

This book is dedicated to every young man and woman who has ever felt alone, forgotten, or unsure of their worth.

To those behind bars and those walking free—

to the student trying to find purpose in a noisy world, and to the child growing up without a father or mother figure to give guidance, comfort, reassurance, understanding, and support—

this is for you.

You may not have had someone to tell you that you matter, but I'm here to remind you: **you were born for more.**

More than your pain.

More than your mistakes.

More than the world's expectations.

May these pages become the voice of hope you've been searching for—

the reminder that God is still writing your story,

and that the Holy Ghost is ready to walk with you, teach you, and strengthen you for what's ahead.

You are not forgotten.

You are not forsaken.

You were born for more.

Preface

I didn't write this book to impress you.

I wrote it because I know what it feels like to be lost, angry, or unsure of who you are.

I know what it means to look for answers in all the wrong places and come up empty.

I've lived long enough to see that many of our young people are not broken beyond repair—they're just unmentored, unloved, and unseen.

Some are behind bars.

Some are in classrooms.

Some are sitting quietly in church pews with smiles that hide the pain they carry inside.

But no matter where you are, I want you to hear me clearly: **You were born for more.**

I've watched generation after generation of young people fall to the same traps—lies that say, *"You'll never change,"* or *"You're not enough."*

The devil doesn't need to destroy you if he can just confuse you. He'll distract you with entertainment, drain you with disappointment, and convince you that your mistakes are final.

But I'm here to tell you, as someone who's been through my own storms—God still has a plan for your life.

This book is a journey of faith, mentorship, and purpose.

It's for the ones who are trying to make sense of their pain, who need guidance when life feels too heavy, and who long for a mentor but don't know where to find one.

You'll find truth here, but also grace.

You'll find correction, but also compassion.

And above all, you'll find *hope*—the kind that only comes from the **Holy Ghost**, who restores what life tried to steal.

Whether you grew up without a father or mother, whether you're sitting in a cell or sitting in class, this message is for you.

You were created by God for a purpose far greater than your surroundings.

And no matter how many times you've fallen, He's still calling you higher.

My prayer is that as you turn these pages, something inside you wakes up.

That the same Spirit who changed my life will begin to stir within yours.

That you will come to know—deep down—that your story isn't over, your dreams aren't dead, and your destiny is still alive in Christ.

So, take this journey one page at a time.

Open your heart.

Ask God to meet you where you are.

And remember:

You were born for more.

— Elder Joel Latimore Jr.

Mission Statement:

This book is written to reach the broken, the forgotten, and the misdirected — especially young men and women who grew up without guidance, structure, or hope.

It exists to remind them that their mistakes do not define them, their pain does not disqualify them, and their story is not over. Through faith, mentorship, and the love of God, they can rise again, rebuild their lives, and discover that they were born for more than what they've become.

Introduction

We were born into systems that promised to protect us—but most of them failed.

They failed our fathers and mothers, and now they're failing our sons and daughters.

We've learned how to survive inside broken systems, but few have been taught how to live beyond them.

The Family

The breakdown began at home. Where there was once structure, there is now struggle.

Where fathers once led with strength and mothers nurtured with wisdom, many homes now fight just to hold together.

Too many children are growing up without the guidance, comfort, reassurance, understanding, and support that once came from family.

The television became the teacher, social media became the mentor, and pain became the voice that shaped identity.

We are now raising generations that have never seen stability—and because they've never seen it, they no longer believe it's possible.

The Church

Then came the silence of the church.

The same institution that once held our communities together began to lose its prophetic voice. The altar became a stage. Worship became performance.

And instead of transforming lives, many churches settled for entertaining crowds.

We talked about blessings but neglected brokenness.

We preached prosperity while ignoring pain.

We created programs but forgot about people.

As a result, the power of the Holy Ghost—the very force that sustained our ancestors through slavery, segregation, and systemic injustice—was pushed aside for comfort and convenience.

We lost fire, and with it, we lost focus.

Education

Our schools, once seen as pathways to liberation, became factories of frustration. A system designed to enlighten began to label, segregate, and exclude.

Gifted minds were overlooked because they didn't fit the mold. Discipline replaced mentorship, and punishment replaced understanding.

Teachers tried their best, but many were unprepared to deal with children who carried trauma in their backpacks and hunger in their hearts.

Instead of cultivating leaders, our schools began producing dropouts—young people who stopped believing education had anything to offer them.

Incarceration

The prison system grew while hope shrank.

Policies like *"three strikes"* and *"mandatory minimums"* swept through our communities like modern-day slavery, locking up fathers before they could raise their sons and disciplining boys before they had the chance to become men.

Jails became warehouses for the wounded— places where potential was buried alive.

Instead of healing trauma, the system hardened it.

Instead of teaching accountability, it produced anger.

And when our young men and women came home, they came home to a world that had already decided who they were.

The Community

Once upon a time, the community was our safety net. Neighbors corrected children who weren't their own.

Elders shared wisdom. Everyone looked out for everyone else.

But somewhere along the way, we stopped being a village and started living as strangers.

The spirit of unity was replaced by isolation. Now, our streets are filled with fear instead of fellowship, competition instead of compassion, and silence instead of support.

The community was never meant to be divided by *envy, violence, and distrust*—but that's exactly what happens when **love disappears.**

A broken community leaves its young people unprotected, searching for belonging in all the wrong places.

Social Neglect

Beyond the walls of family, church, and school, society itself turned cold.

Communities were stripped of *jobs, dignity, and direction.*

Poverty became normal.

Media began to *glorify violence, rebellion, and promiscuity*—selling lies dressed up as success.

The village that once raised children was replaced by a digital crowd that mocks truth and rewards foolishness. Many of our young people now live with full phones but empty hearts.

The Failure of Moral Upbringing

At the heart of all these failures lies the loss of moral upbringing.

There was a time when children were taught to *respect their elders, honor authority, tell the truth, and work with integrity.*

There was a time when we prayed before meals, quoted Scripture before bed, and were reminded that **"God is watching."**

Those lessons-built character—they created men and women who stood for something, even when life was hard.

But somewhere along the way, we stopped teaching morals and started teaching excuses.

We told our children they could *"be whatever they want to be,"* but we didn't tell them they would answer to God for whatever they became.

We taught ambition without accountability, freedom without boundaries, and expression without discipline.

As a result, many of our young people grew up gifted but directionless, talented but spiritually empty.

When the home stopped teaching right from wrong, the streets stepped in.

When fathers stopped correcting, gangs started recruiting.

When mothers stopped praying, social media started preaching.

When the church stopped crying out for holiness, the world filled the silence with compromise.

And when the community stopped caring, the children stopped believing.

This is not just a crisis of poverty or policy—it is a crisis of morality.

We have raised generations who know how to make money but not how to manage temptation.

We have children who can build businesses but cannot build character.

And in the absence of moral training, chaos has become normal. A moral foundation doesn't begin in the courthouse; it begins in the living room. It begins with *parents who teach respect, mentors who model integrity, and churches that preach righteousness instead of popularity.*

Without moral training, every other form of education becomes dangerous, because knowledge without wisdom leads to destruction.

The enemy knows this.

That's why he fights to destroy the family, silence the church, corrupt the schools, fracture the community, and distort the media—because if he can break our moral compass, he can steer our children anywhere he wants even to Hell.

The Truth and the Hope

All these systems—family, church, community, education, incarceration, and society—were meant to serve us.

But when we abandoned God, those systems turned against us. They can't heal what only the Spirit can restore.

And until faith returns to the center of our communities, we will keep repeating the same cycles of pain.

This book was written to confront those cycles.

It is a call to awaken purpose, restore mentorship, and bring the Holy Ghost back to the next generation. We can't rebuild the world overnight, but we can start by rebuilding people—one life at a time.

So, whether you are free or incarcerated, male or female, in school or on the streets, this message is for you.

God hasn't forgotten about you.

You were born for more—and now it's time to rise into it.

— **Elder Joel Latimore Jr.**

Why Black Youth Need Mentoring

Our youth are crying out for guidance—some with their voices, others through their silence.

They may not say it out loud, but *their choices, their pain, and their confusion* reveal it every day. They are searching for *direction, affirmation, and love* in a world that has taught them how to survive, but not how to live.

For generations, Black youth have carried the weight of broken systems—*family, church, school, and society*—all of which were meant to nurture them but instead neglected them. The results are devastating: *a crisis of identity, purpose, and faith.*

We see it in the headlines, in our classrooms, and on our streets. But this is not simply a social issue—it is **a spiritual emergency.**

1. A Crisis of Identity

When fathers disappear and mothers grow weary, when the church falls silent and the community stops caring, confusion takes root.

Many young men and women no longer know who they are or what they were created to be. They imitate what they see because no one is present to show them who they truly are.

Without mentors, they become products of their environment instead of reflections of God's image. That is why so many chase after *titles, trends, and temporary validation*—trying to fill a void that only purpose can satisfy.

2. Broken Families, Broken Foundations

- In 2023, nearly **49.7 % of Black children** lived in households with only one parent, compared with about **20.2 % of white children.** OJJDP

- According to the Current Population Survey, **only 37 % of Black children** live with their two biological parents, **while 48 %** live in single-parent homes. Institute for Family Studies

- Some reports also state that around **66 % of Black children are being raised in single-parent homes,** compared to about **24 % of white children.** DefenderNetwork.com

That statistic isn't just a number—it's a wound. It means that too many young people are growing up without fathers to affirm them or stable households *to model responsibility, balance, and godly discipline.* Mothers have fought valiantly to hold the line, but the burden was never meant to be carried alone.

When the family breaks, identity breaks. And when identity breaks, the enemy rushes in to define what only God can define.

3. The Silence of the Church

The church that once held our people together has, in many places, lost its prophetic voice. The altar became a stage, and worship became performance.

Instead of transforming souls, we often settled for entertaining crowds. As a result, the very institution that once raised strong men and women of faith now struggles to reach the next generation.

The Holy Ghost was never meant to be replaced by programs. When the church loses fire, the community loses focus. **Mentorship is the bridge that reconnects the two.**

4. Schools Without Mentors

Education was once the key to freedom for Black people, but now many of our children walk into schools carrying trauma no textbook can heal.

They are *disciplined* when they need to be understood, *labeled* when they need to be loved, and *ignored* when they need to be inspired.

Too few teachers see them as leaders in training; too many see them as problems to manage. **Mentorship** turns those classrooms back into gardens—places where potential is watered and faith is cultivated.

Relevant Statistics:

- Black students represented about **15 %** of the student population in 2015–16—but accounted for **31 %** of in-school arrests or referrals to law enforcement. American Bar Association +2

- In K–12 settings, Black children are **3.8 times** more likely to be suspended or removed from class than their white peers. floodcenter.org

- Black males are four times more likely to be suspended than their peers. PMC

- Around **5 %** of white students are suspended or expelled during their K–12 years, compared with **16 %** of Black students. Education Week

- Each additional suspension significantly increases the odds of incarceration over time. PMC

These disparities show that punishment and exclusion have become default responses—fields where mentorship could have *intervened, healed, or redirected.*

5. The Rise of False Mentorship

When home and church fall silent, culture steps in to teach.

Music, movies, and social media have become modern pulpits, *shaping values, identities, and desires.* Rappers, influencers, and celebrities now mentor our youth—preaching *rebellion, lust, greed, and pride.*

The tragedy is that these idols look strong while dying inside. They sell *struggle without salvation.* They preach *"realness" but not righteousness.*

We've raised a generation that knows how to go viral, but not how to be *virtuous*. What entertains them eventually enters them. And what enters them soon defines them.

6. The Loss of Moral Compass

This generation was not just misled—it was unmentored.

They were taught ambition without accountability, expression without discipline, and freedom without boundaries. Knowledge increased, but wisdom decreased.

We told them they could be anything they wanted to be, but we didn't teach them who God wanted them to be.

The absence of mentorship left a spiritual vacuum that no government program or social reform can fill. Because the problem is not only economic—*it's moral. It's spiritual.*

7. The Call to Rebuild

God is calling us back to the basics—to raise up **mentors** *who will stand in the gap, model righteousness, and restore what the enemy has stolen.*

Our youth don't just need correction; they need *connection*. They don't just need rules; they need *relationship.* **Mentorship** provides both—it teaches truth with compassion and discipline with love.

Every child deserves a voice that believes in them, a hand that guides them, and a heart that won't give up on them.

This is why mentorship matters.

Because one relationship can break a generational curse.

One godly mentor can rewrite a destiny.

And one act of love can restore a lost identity.

Our sons and daughters were never meant to be statistics.

They were born to be leaders, prophets, builders, and dreamers.

They were born for more.

Reflective Summary:

The need for mentorship among Black youth is not just social—it is spiritual. The family has cracked, the church has grown silent, and culture has grown loud.

Mentorship is God's way of restoring what has been lost. It repairs identity, renews purpose, and redirects potential.

When a mentor steps into a young person's life, heaven makes an investment in earth.

And when a young man or woman finally realizes that they are not forgotten—that they are seen, valued, and called—the chains of confusion begin to break.

We cannot rebuild the world until we rebuild people.

And we cannot rebuild people until we reach their hearts through mentorship rooted in the Holy Ghost, truth, and love.

This is how revival begins—*one soul, one conversation, one relationship at a time.*

Prayer for Mentorship and Restoration:

Heavenly Father,

Thank You for reminding us that the next generation is not lost—they are waiting to be led.

Forgive us for the times we were silent when we should have spoken, distant when we should have drawn near, and judgmental when we should have shown mercy.

Lord, raise up mentors filled with wisdom, patience, and compassion.

Teach us to see potential where others see problems, and to love these young men and women the way You loved us—unconditionally.

Restore the broken homes, revive the sleeping churches, and renew the strength of our communities.

Help every child know that they were born for more—that You have a plan, a purpose, and a future for their lives.

Use us, Lord, to be lights in dark places and examples of what grace can do.

In Jesus' name we pray. Amen.

Chapter 1 – The Crisis of Lost Identity

"Be not deceived: evil communications corrupt good manners." — **1 Corinthians 15:33 (KJV)**

Mentorship as a Need—Why Youth Require Guidance and Direction

This chapter is for you—the one who has ever felt invisible, forgotten, or unsure of who you are anymore.

Maybe you grew up without direction, or life's disappointments made you question your worth. You've tried to fit in, tried to survive, but deep inside you know this isn't all there is.

You were created for more than the pain you've been living through.

When **Paul** wrote these words to the Corinthians, he warned believers not to underestimate the power of influence. Corruption rarely begins overnight; it begins with conversation.

The voices you listen to shape the choices you make. *"Evil communications"* means more than foul language—it means corrupted influence and ungodly company. *"Good manners"* points to *character, discipline, and spiritual integrity.*

Our generation swims in communication—phones, posts, podcasts—but often drowns in confusion. With all this connection, conviction is fading.

The voices shaping our youth are no longer parents or pastors, but entertainers and algorithms that care nothing for their souls.

Young men imitate rappers who glorify rebellion; **young women** copy influencers who worship vanity.

- If you **listen** long enough to lies, you start mistaking them for truth.

- If you **walk** with those who despise discipline, you begin to reject correction.

- If you **celebrate** sin, holiness starts to feel outdated.

When fathers are absent and mothers are weary, when the Church grows silent and the streets grow loud, *"evil communications"* fill the gap.

That's why mentorship matters—it replaces bad company with *good guidance*, empty talk with **godly counsel.**

Broken Fathers and Silent Voices

So many wounds begin at home.

Perhaps your father wasn't there, or if he was, he didn't know how to love.

Some of you were raised by strong mothers who carried too much, while others had no consistent voice of love at all.

Without guidance, the heart searches for approval anywhere it can find it—on the streets, online, or in the arms of those who use you.

If that's your story, hear this truth: **God has not abandoned you.**

He is the Father to the fatherless and still calls you by name.

Your value doesn't come from who raised you but from who created you.

When fathers disappear, families fracture; when families fracture, direction is lost—but even then, God begins rebuilding worth piece by piece.

Broken Systems, Broken Souls

Communities traded wisdom for convenience.

Schools teach skills but not character; the streets offer belonging but hide the cost.

Even churches sometimes grow quiet when the world needs their cry for righteousness.

Maybe you've already felt those failures. The people who should have protected you ended up hurting you.

But remember—you can rise from broken systems. You don't have to repeat the pattern you were born into.

We replaced fathers with welfare checks, discipline with distraction, and rewarded brokenness instead of rebuilding order.

Government programs can feed bodies but not restore purpose.

Education and money have value, but only God's Word builds identity that lasts.

"Man shall not live by bread alone, but by every word that proceedeth out of the mouth of God."
— Matthew 4:4

When guidance disappears at home or in the community, many young people turn to social media to fill the silence. What the world fails to teach, the media quickly replaces—and not always for good.

The Power of Media and False Mentorship

When home fails, the world becomes the teacher.

Music, movies, and social media now disciple a generation.

They preach rebellion as freedom and lust as love, but every promise has a price.

"Love not the world… for all that is in the world, the lust of the flesh, and the lust of the eyes, and the pride of life, is not of the Father." — **1 John 2:15-16**

We live in a culture raised by entertainers instead of elders.

When fathers vanished, the culture sent replacements—men with **microphones** instead of morals and women with **fame** instead of faith.

The result?

Followers without direction.

Music isn't the enemy—the message is.

What entertains you eventually enters you.

Feed on rebellion and it will consume you.

Yet there is hope: the same God who redeems the addict can redeem the artist. He can raise up a generation whose rhythm carries righteousness and whose lyrics lead to life.

Identity Theft: The Enemy's Oldest Trick

The devil's greatest weapon has always been deception.

If he can steal your perception, he can control your direction.

Forget who you are, and you'll act like what you're not.

Psychologist Erik Erikson taught that human identity develops in stages—from *trust in infancy to autonomy, initiative, industry, and finally identity in adolescence.*

Each stage depends on loving guidance.

When trust is broken, fear takes root.

When autonomy is mocked, shame grows.

When initiative is crushed, guilt appears.

When industry is ignored, feelings of inferiority form.

And when identity is never affirmed, confusion becomes the norm.

That's why so many young people struggle today—not just because of culture, but because the early building blocks of confidence and belonging were never set in place.

As I often say, *confusion attracts destruction.*

Mentorship restores what confusion destroys. It replaces imitation with direction and teaches that your past doesn't define your potential.

A Call to Rebuild

We can't let statistics write our story. Every child deserves a model of faith, a voice of wisdom, and an example of strength.

The government may not fix it, but God's people can redeem it—one relationship at a time.

Paul wrote, *"Fathers, provoke not your children to wrath: but bring them up in the nurture and admonition of the Lord."* — **Ephesians 6:4**

That verse holds two keys: **nurture** and **admonition**—**love** and **discipline.**

Children need both. **Love** without guidance creates entitlement; **guidance** without love breeds resentment.

Parents, mentors, and communities share the same assignment: raise children in an environment where truth and tenderness walk together.

Erikson reminded us that growth continues through life; damaged stages can be healed through new trust, purpose, and identity.

Spiritually, that's what the Church is for—to become a family where broken foundations are rebuilt.

Every generation rises or falls by the presence of **mentors** who care enough to correct and guide.

Real change begins when someone decides to stand in the gap—to become *the father figure, the encourager, or the spiritual example* that others never had.

"If the foundations be destroyed, what can the righteous do?" — **Psalm 11:3**

The answer: *we rebuild. We mentor. We teach. We reflect Christ.*

Closing Charge

You were not born to be a statistic.

You were born for significance.

Even if no one taught you who you are, heaven already knows your name.

You are more than a product of your environment—**you are a purpose in progress.**

If no one ever told you before, let me be the first: **You were born for more.**

Reflective Questions:

1. Who or what has shaped your identity most up to this point?

2. How have false influences affected your choices or confidence?

3. What mentors—positive or negative—have guided your path?

4. In what area do you sense God calling you to rebuild?

5. How can you begin showing the same guidance to someone else?

Reflective Summary:

Every broken system begins with a broken person, but every healed person can rebuild a system.

Identity is not found in culture; it's found in Christ.

When you let God redefine who you are, the lies of your past lose power.

You were never forgotten—only unfinished.

And He who began a good work in you will complete it.

Prayer for Repentance and Forgiveness:

Heavenly Father,

I confess that I've searched for identity in the wrong places.

Forgive me for listening to voices that pulled me from You.

Heal the wounds of my past—restore my trust, my confidence, and my purpose.

Teach me to live by Your Word and surround me with mentors who reflect Your love.

Help me become the example someone else needs to see.

In Jesus' name, Amen.

Chapter 2 – The Power of Guidance: Why We All Need a Mentor

"Where no counsel is, the people fall: but in the multitude of counsellors there is safety."

— **Proverbs 11:14 (KJV)**

Mentorship as Discipleship — Learning to Receive Direction

We live in a generation that often confuses independence with wisdom.

Everybody wants to lead, but few are willing to be led.

Many young men and women believe that needing guidance makes them weak—but the truth is, **guidance** is what keeps us from destruction.

No one rises alone. No one matures without accountability. No one fulfills purpose without direction.

Even the most powerful men and women in Scripture had someone *to correct them, sharpen them, and show them how to walk before God with integrity.*

"He that walketh with wise men shall be wise: but a companion of fools shall be destroyed."

— Proverbs 13:20

That means your destiny is tied to your direction—and your direction is shaped by the company you keep.

You may have been taught that asking for help makes you small, but learning to receive help is where strength begins.

Even the strongest believers need someone to help them see what they cannot see.

The Need for Guidance

Many of us were raised to survive, not to listen.

Some came from homes where anger spoke louder than instruction, where fathers were absent and mothers were overwhelmed.

Others grew up trusting no one but themselves.

But survival is not the same as success—it only keeps you breathing, not growing.

Without spiritual direction, survival can become self-destruction.

The enemy loves isolation. He whispers, *"No one understands you; you're better off alone."*

But isolation drains strength. You were created to walk with others.

Every person who ever accomplished something great had someone to guide them:

- **Moses had Jethro.**

- **Joshua had Moses.**

- **Elisha had Elijah.**

- **The Apostles had Jesus.**

- **Timothy had Paul.**

The pattern is clear: those who walk alone stumble sooner, but those who walk with the wise stand stronger.

Why Guidance Matters — What Psychology and Scripture Agree On

The need for guidance is written into both the soul and the science of human growth.

God designed us to need *relationship, direction, and affirmation* as we grow.

Erik Erikson, a noted developmental psychologist, taught that the first stage of human development is learning **trust versus mistrust.**

If a child does not experience consistent love and guidance early in life, trust becomes difficult later.

Many of today's young men and women are not rebellious by nature—they are simply responding to years of disappointment.

They long for direction, but life taught them not to trust anyone enough to receive it.

That's why mentorship is not optional; it's a lifeline.

When a mentor steps in with *patience, love, and godly correction,* they help rebuild what neglect tore down: *the ability to trust, to listen, and to believe in one's own value again.*

Abraham Maslow, another psychologist, described human motivation as a hierarchy of needs—starting with *safety, belonging, and self-esteem before reaching one's highest potential.*

If those early needs are ignored, a person struggles to mature, no matter how old they are.

Mentorship meets those God-given needs—it provides **belonging** where there was rejection, **wisdom** where there was confusion, and **security** where there was fear.

That's why **Paul** charged parents to *"bring [their children] up in the nurture and admonition of the Lord"* **(Ephesians 6:4).**

When a family, church, or community fails to **nurture** and **instruct**, children grow up seeking validation in the wrong places—on the streets, on screens, or in the arms of deception.

Guidance fills that void with purpose.

It says, *"You still matter, and there is a better way."*

God's Design for Guidance

Mentorship is not man's idea—it is God's design.

From the very beginning, God modeled it. He walked with Adam in the cool of the day, teaching him how to live.

He gave Israel the Law through Moses so they would have direction.

He sent prophets to warn kings, and He sent His Son, Jesus Christ, to model perfect obedience.

Guidance was never meant to control you—it was meant to complete you.

When you reject instruction, you block your own growth. When you receive it, you unlock destiny.

"Hear counsel, and receive instruction, that thou mayest be wise in thy latter end."
— Proverbs 19:20

If you listen now, you'll thank God later.

True mentorship isn't about someone telling you who to be; it's about discovering who you already are in God.

A real mentor doesn't compete with you—they help complete what's missing in your maturity.

The Trap of Pride

Pride has a thousand disguises. It can sound like confidence but act like rebellion.

It says, *"I don't need advice; I know what I'm doing."*

Yet the same pride that promises freedom quietly builds prisons of failure.

Maybe you've been hurt by people who tried to control or criticize you, and now pride feels like protection.

But walls that keep pain out also keep healing out.

God isn't trying to restrict you—He's trying to restore you.

You can't correct what you refuse to face, and you can't grow beyond the wisdom you reject.

If you're tired of going in circles, it's time to open your heart again.

The Bible says, *"Without counsel purposes are disappointed: but in the multitude of counsellors they are established."*
  — Proverbs 15:22

Purpose dies without instruction; dreams collapse without direction.

Learning to Trust Again

Some of us stopped trusting after betrayal. Parents, pastors, or friends may have failed you, leaving you suspicious of anyone claiming to care.

But God is not like man. When others walk away, He steps closer.

When others speak carelessly, He speaks with compassion.

Through **the Holy Ghost**, God becomes the ultimate Mentor. He not only corrects you—He comforts you.

He not only teaches truth—He walks you through it.

Jesus promised, *"When he, the Spirit of truth, is come, he will guide you into all truth."*

— John 16:13

If you've ever felt lost, know this: **God has not given up on you.**

He still wants to lead you—but He will not drag you; you must choose to follow.

When you open your heart to Him, He will also send trustworthy people—*mentors, pastors, or elders*—to confirm His direction.

They aren't perfect, but they can help you see what's ahead and remind you that you're not walking alone.

The Blessing of Wise Company

You were never meant to walk this journey called life alone.

There is wisdom in walking with those who have already faced the battles you are trying to win.

The right company will not only encourage your gifts—they will challenge your growth.

They will see greatness in you when you cannot see it in yourself.

"Iron sharpeneth iron; so a man sharpeneth the countenance of his friend."

— **Proverbs 27:17**

Growth happens through **accountability**. The same way iron creates sparks when sharpened, your character is refined through **relationship**.

Sometimes that friction feels uncomfortable, but correction is not rejection—it's protection.

- If you surround yourself with the wise, you will rise.

- If you surround yourself with fools, you will fall.

The choice is yours—but your future depends on it.

Reflective Questions:

1. Who are the voices you listen to most, and where are they leading you?

2. Have past disappointments made it hard for you to trust spiritual guidance?

3. What might change if you let God teach you through someone again?

4. Can you recognize any patterns of pride that keep you from receiving help?

5. What step can you take today to become more teachable and connected?

Reflective Summary:

We were not created to walk alone. Guidance is not weakness; it is wisdom.

Every strong leader was once a humble learner. Every mentor was once a student who chose to listen.

When you reject counsel, you delay destiny.

When you receive correction with a pure heart, you grow *stronger, wiser, and more stable in your walk with God.*

The power of guidance is that it turns **information** into **transformation.**

It teaches that independence without wisdom leads to failure, but submission to truth leads to freedom.

Let **the Holy Ghost** be your first Teacher, and let godly mentors help shape your journey—because one day, God will use you to do the same for someone else.

Prayer for Guidance and Humility:

Heavenly Father,

Thank You for being my Teacher, my Guide, and my Protector. Forgive me for the times I ignored wisdom or tried to make it on my own.

Heal my trust and soften my heart to receive direction again. Place godly voices around me and give me discernment to recognize them.

Remove pride, rebellion, and fear from my spirit. Surround me with wise people who will sharpen and strengthen me.

And when the time comes, teach me how to guide others with love and truth.

In Jesus' name, Amen.

Chapter 3 – Learning to Follow Before You Lead

"Whosoever will be chief among you, let him be your servant." — **Matthew 20:27 (KJV)**

The Truth About Leadership

True leadership doesn't begin with a title—it begins with a towel. Before God entrusts anyone with authority, He first teaches them humility.

In a world obsessed with platforms, followers, and influence, God is still looking for servants. Our generation has confused visibility with value. Many want to be known before they've been proven.

But in God's Kingdom, the way up is still down. You cannot lead others where you have never been led, and you cannot teach obedience if you have never learned submission.

- **Before David ever ruled Israel, he served Saul.**

- **Before Elisha performed miracles, he poured water on Elijah's hands.**

- **Before Joseph wore a crown, he wore chains.**

Every anointed leader must pass through the classroom of following.

1. The Lost Art of Submission

Submission is a word few want to hear. Our culture equates it with weakness, but in the Kingdom of God, it is a mark of strength. True submission isn't about control—it's about trust. It's about yielding to God's order even when it doesn't make sense.

Many young believers struggle with authority because they have seen it abused. Some were raised by controlling parents or manipulated by leaders who confused servanthood with slavery.

Yet *rebellion, distrust, and pride* are just as dangerous as domination. They block spiritual growth and delay destiny.

When you refuse to submit to godly authority, you limit how much God can entrust to you.

David refused to harm Saul even when Saul tried to kill him.

Why?

Because he understood that the same hand that lifted Saul up could also bring him down. **Promotion comes from God**—not man.

Submission doesn't mean silence in the face of sin; it means waiting for God's timing rather than taking matters into your own hands. The one who learns to follow well becomes the one God can trust to lead well.

2. Servanthood: The Foundation of Leadership

Jesus gave the perfect example in **John 13** when He took a towel, knelt before His disciples, and washed their feet. The Lord of glory became the servant of all. He said, *"If I then, your Lord and Master, have washed your feet; ye also ought to wash one another's feet."*

The secret to promotion in God's Kingdom is **humility** and **faithfulness.** Before you can lead people, **you must first learn to serve them.**

Many want the platform but not the process. Yet God watches how you handle the small things. **Luke 16:10** reminds us, *"He that is faithful in that which is least is faithful also in much."*

If you can serve without recognition, God can trust you with responsibility. If you can honor others when no one honors you, God can use you to build His Kingdom.

Servanthood doesn't make you less—it prepares you for more. The towel is the training ground for the throne.

3. The Process of Preparation

Every true leader endures three seasons before the promise: **the wilderness, the waiting,** and **the working.**

The **wilderness** tests your heart when no one is watching.

The **waiting** tests your patience when nothing seems to be happening.

The **working** tests your faithfulness when no one applauds your effort.

David served Saul before he ever fought Goliath. **Joseph** was faithful in prison before he was promoted in Pharaoh's palace. These men didn't rush the process—they trusted it.

The wilderness doesn't destroy true leaders; it defines them. *It purifies motives, strips pride, and clarifies purpose.* The process may be painful, but it's always purposeful—God uses it to prepare you for the weight of what's ahead.

Modern research confirms what Scripture has shown all along. The human brain, particularly the **prefrontal cortex**—the area responsible for *decision-making, foresight, and emotional balance*—develops gradually as a person matures.

That's why God often takes years to prepare His servants.

Joseph's life reflects that divine design. In his youth, he dreamed greatly but spoke unwisely.

His gift was strong, but his judgment was still forming. Through *betrayal, servanthood, and imprisonment,* Joseph's mind and spirit matured together. Each act of obedience rewired his thinking and strengthened his discernment.

By the time Pharaoh summoned him, Joseph's *heart was steady, his mind disciplined, and his words measured.* He had learned to **think** before speaking, to **trust** before reacting, and to **serve** before ruling. His years of hidden obedience shaped both his brain and his character.

When Joseph stood before Pharaoh, he was not the same young dreamer who once sought attention—he was a seasoned man whose wisdom had been born through suffering and shaped through service. When his mind was ready, his purpose was revealed.

4. How to Follow Well

Learning to follow well means learning to trust God even when people fail. It means respecting authority even when leadership is imperfect.

Hebrews 13:17 instructs, *"Obey them that have the rule over you, and submit yourselves: for they watch for your souls."*

The problem isn't that we lack leaders—it's that too many followers are unteachable. The greatest test of character is how you handle correction.

Do you grow from it or get offended by it?

The blessing of following well is that it protects you. When you remain in position until God says move, you are covered by His timing.

Don't abandon your post because it feels uncomfortable. Growth often hides in the uncomfortable places.

5. From Following to Leading

When the time is right, God will elevate the faithful. The moment of promotion will come suddenly—but not prematurely. Every lesson learned in servanthood becomes the foundation for leadership.

Following teaches *discipline, empathy, patience, and wisdom*. It teaches you how to handle *people, pressure, and purpose.* When God finally opens the door, you'll understand that leadership isn't about power—it's about people. It's about serving with *compassion* and leading with *humility.*

Every true leader remembers where they came from. They don't forget those who *trained, corrected, or believed in them* when no one else did. The same hands that once held a towel will one day carry a crown—but the towel must come first.

Reflective Questions:

1. What areas of your life has God called you to serve before He promotes you?

2. Have you ever resisted authority because of past hurt or misunderstanding?

3. How do you respond to correction—defensively or with humility?

4. Are you willing to follow even when the leader isn't perfect?

5. What has God been teaching you in your current "waiting season"?

Reflective Summary:

True leadership is born in hidden places. Before God can use your voice publicly, He will test your obedience privately.

Following is not a delay of destiny—it is divine preparation. Every great leader was once a faithful follower who chose **humility** over haste, **patience** over pride, and **service** over status.

When you serve with integrity and wait on God's timing, promotion will find you. Remember, in the Kingdom, crowns are earned through **calloused hands,** not clever words.

Prayer for Obedience and Humility:

Heavenly Father,

Thank You for reminding me that leadership begins with servanthood. Teach me to follow You with humility and to honor those You've placed over me.

Remove rebellion, pride, and impatience from my heart. Help me learn from correction and serve faithfully wherever You have planted me.

Prepare my spirit for greater responsibility, and when You choose to elevate me, let me never forget that I am first and always Your servant.

In Jesus' name, Amen.

Chapter 4 – When God Develops You in Secret

(Understanding Hidden Seasons and Divine Silence)

"He that dwelleth in the secret place of the most High shall abide under the shadow of the Almighty." — **Psalm 91:1 (KJV)**

The Hidden Place of Growth

Every calling has a classroom, and God's classroom is often hidden.

You may feel *unseen, overlooked, or forgotten*—but in the Kingdom, what looks like isolation is often preparation.

When God develops you in secret, He is not punishing you; *He is protecting your process.*

The soil must stay dark for the seed to grow. The seed doesn't complain about the dirt—it trusts that something greater is forming beneath the surface.

In the same way, God buries potential so it can take root before it bears fruit.

Many mistake silence for absence, but God's silence is often His way of saying, *"Stay still— I'm shaping you."*

He **hides** you to heal you, **delays** you to mature you, and **withholds visibility** so your character can catch up to your calling.

The Pattern of Hidden Seasons

Every great man or woman of God experienced a season of obscurity before destiny unfolded.

- **Joseph** served in prison before ruling in Pharaoh's palace.

- **Moses** spent forty years in the desert before leading Israel.

- **David** was anointed as king but sent back to tend sheep.

- **Jesus** spent thirty quiet years before three years of ministry.

If God allowed them to be developed in secret, He will do the same for you.

Hidden seasons teach what public stages cannot—they reveal whether you will serve faithfully when no one is watching.

It's in secret places that God removes the noise of other voices so you can hear His clearly.

The Purpose of Silence

Divine silence is not rejection—**it's redirection**.

When God hides you, He's tuning your heart to hear Him alone.

Sometimes He closes every door you try to open because the next stage requires a new version of you.

You cannot step into purpose with the same habits or insecurity that once held you back.

In silence, God strips away your need for applause and teaches you to depend on His approval.

He shows you that peace comes not from being seen, but from being secure in His will.

Isaiah 30:15 reminds us, *"In quietness and in confidence shall be your strength."*

When everything feels quiet, it's not the end of your story—it's the strengthening of your spirit.

The Cave of Development

When David fled from Saul, he found himself in the cave of Adullam **(1 Samuel 22).** He had been anointed for greatness but forced into hiding. The crown was promised, yet nowhere in sight. What seemed like punishment was actually preparation.

Inside that dark cave, something divine took place. David wasn't surrounded by royalty—he was joined by *the distressed, the indebted, and the discontented.* Those were not soldiers; they were broken men. But under David's guidance, they became mighty warriors.

The cave became God's classroom where a leader learned to transform pain into **purpose** and isolation into **influence.**

That is how God mentors' future leaders. He trains them in confinement, not comfort. When you are *hidden, misunderstood, or confined by life's circumstances,* God is shaping you for greater influence.

He teaches you to serve without applause, to lead without a title, and to trust Him when the next step isn't clear.

Every *"cave"* in your life—whether it's a small apartment, a hospital room, or a season of unemployment—can become your Adullam if you let God use it.

In the silence of that place, He *forges character, builds resilience, and teaches you how to see others through eyes of compassion.*

Many of the men who entered that cave with David were lost and hopeless, but they emerged as champions because they followed a man who first learned how to follow God in solitude.

Modern mentorship follows the same pattern: transformation happens not in the spotlight but in the secret places where humility is forged and faith is refined.

Just as David's cave became the training ground for kingship, **your private struggles are preparing you for public purpose.** What feels like restriction today may be the very environment God uses to reveal the leader He placed inside you.

The Blessing of Divine Delay

Waiting seasons are not wasted seasons. When God delays, He is developing you.

He teaches **patience** through delay, **discipline** through denial, and **dependence** through stillness.

Every moment of waiting is an investment in wisdom. The longer Joseph served in the shadows, the stronger his character became. By the time he stood before Pharaoh, he was ready—not just anointed, but anchored.

Delays are not denials—they are divine appointments with growth.

Growth Through God's Design

Modern psychology agrees that growth takes time.

Erik Erikson taught that trust and stability form the foundation of identity, while **Abraham Maslow** described *self-actualization* as the highest human need.

Yet in God's Kingdom, this becomes ***Christ-actualization***—becoming who He created you to be through *trust, discipline, and hidden obedience.*

When God hides you, He is strengthening the spiritual *"muscles"* of patience, discernment, and endurance.

He is building **internal confidence** before **external recognition.**

What the world calls stagnation, Heaven calls sanctification.

Modern psychology also reminds us that the shaping of identity is never neutral.

Dr. William E. Cross Jr., who studied Black identity development, taught that self-understanding grows through stages—first confusion, then discovery, then internal peace.

In hidden seasons, God often walks us through those same stages, replacing confusion with clarity and pain with purpose.

And as **Dr. Mamie Phipps Clark** showed in her research with children, early messages about worth can shape a lifetime of belief.

That is why divine mentorship matters so deeply: God speaks truth to the places where the world once whispered inferiority.

The Discipline of Stillness

Stillness is one of God's greatest tools.

Psalm 46:10 says, *"Be still, and know that I am God."*

You cannot know His power until you stop fighting His process.

Stillness teaches surrender—it **silences** pride, **calms** fear, and **clarifies** direction.

When you stop striving to be seen, you start hearing what God has been saying all along.

Learning to be still is part of learning to trust.

Those who rush ahead miss the revelation meant for those who wait.

Hidden but Not Forgotten

You are not overlooked—you are being observed by Heaven.

God's eye is on you even when no one applauds.

He is measuring how you handle small tasks, quiet seasons, and delayed answers.

Zechariah 4:10 reminds us, *"For who hath despised the day of small things?"*

The small days are sacred days—the ones that test your faith and prove your endurance.

When you're faithful in the shadows, God will trust you with the spotlight.

He develops warriors in caves before He reveals them in battle.

So don't despise your secret place—it's where your strength is being born.

Reflective Questions:

1. Have you ever mistaken God's silence for abandonment?

2. What are you learning about yourself in your current hidden season?

3. How do you respond when no one notices your effort or growth?

4. What small assignments has God given you to prepare for larger ones?

5. How can you trust His timing even when you don't understand His silence?

Reflective Summary:

The hidden season is not a delay—it's divine design.

God hides what He values most. He's shaping your patience, refining your motives, and deepening your trust.

The silence is not punishment—**it's preparation.**

When He finally brings you into the open, you'll realize that every quiet day was a building block for the purpose He's about to reveal. When your hidden season ends, God's next lesson begins— He positions you for purpose.

And when God brings you out of hiding, He brings you into responsibility—because revelation is always followed by assignment.

Prayer for Strength in the Hidden Place:

Heavenly Father,

Thank You for the seasons when You hide me to heal me.

Help me to embrace the silence and trust Your unseen hand.

When I feel forgotten, remind me that You are forming something greater within me.

Teach me to serve faithfully, wait patiently, and grow quietly until You say it's time to be revealed.

May every hidden moment prepare me to represent You well when my season comes.

In Jesus' name, Amen.

Chapter 5 – Positioned for Purpose

How God Uses Redirection to Reveal Destiny

"And we know that all things work together for good to them that love God, to them who are the called according to his purpose."

— Romans 8:28 (KJV)

When God Changes the Route

Every *closed door, delay, or detour* in your life is part of God's mentoring process.

Divine redirection is never random—it's purposeful.

It is the Holy Ghost's way of saying, *"You're ready to grow."*

Many of us panic when plans collapse. We think something went wrong.

But in truth, God is steering us off the highway of comfort onto the narrow road of calling.

What feels like rejection is often redirection.

Even **the Apostle Paul** planned to preach in Asia, yet **Acts 16** says the Holy Ghost forbade him and sent him to Macedonia. That single change opened the gospel to Europe. God's "No" to Asia was His "Yes" to destiny.

Redirection is how God mentors us into maturity.

He changes our route to change our results.

Learning in the Detour

Dr. Myles Munroe once said, *"Purpose is when you know and understand what you were born to accomplish."*

But purpose isn't born in comfort; it's discovered in movement.

Every twist, pause, and disappointment shapes you for destiny.

Psychologist Erik Erikson taught that during youth, people wrestle with identity versus confusion—asking, Who am I? Why am I here?

He noted that *identity* forms through *guidance, community, and trial*—exactly how God grows His children.

Joseph lived this truth.

His brothers' betrayal wasn't punishment—it was placement.

The pit, the prison, and the palace were classrooms.

Each season taught him what privilege never could: *leadership, forgiveness, and faith.*

So, if you feel delayed, remember—delay isn't denial.

You are exactly where God needs you to be.

Psychiatrist Viktor Frankl, who survived the Holocaust, wrote that those who find meaning in suffering endure it best.

Faith teaches the same truth: every painful detour becomes a divine lesson when you let God define it.

When Redirection Feels Like Rejection

Sometimes God's mentorship hurts.

You prayed for a *"yes"* and got silence. You loved deeply and were left empty.

When Jo left, I felt crushed. I had trusted again, believed again, and thought love would last this time.

But in my grief, the Holy Ghost whispered, *"You're not being punished—you're being prepared."*

Later, I understood: had Jo stayed, I might have settled in comfort instead of growing in character.

Her exit was God's entrance into a deeper faith.

What looked like loss was really protection.

God's **"No"** isn't rejection—**it's redirection.**

He removes what limits destiny so that you can mature without distraction.

The Lord mentors through subtraction as well as addition.

Mentorship Through Environment and Example

God also mentors through movement of environment.

Sometimes He shifts your surroundings so you'll meet voices that sharpen you.

When **Ruth** left Moab, she didn't know she was walking toward **Boaz** and into the lineage of **Christ.**

When **David** fled from **Saul,** he found himself in the cave of Adullam—leading broken men who would one day become his mighty warriors. The cave was not punishment; it was preparation.

God trains leaders in confinement, not comfort.

In hidden seasons, you learn to depend on His presence, not applause.

Your cave is where courage is formed.

Sometimes mentorship doesn't come from a person—it comes from the process.

Every new environment, every change of scenery, is God shaping you through *exposure, experience, and endurance.*

Purpose Under Pressure

Pressure is the classroom where purpose matures.

Behavioral psychologist B. F. Skinner discovered that repeated discipline builds strength—he called it **reinforcement.**

Likewise, every trial God allows reinforces obedience.

Hebrews 12:11 says, *"No chastening for the present seemeth joyous, but grievous: nevertheless afterward it yieldeth the peaceable fruit of righteousness."*

In other words, correction hurts before it heals—but it always produces fruit.

Moses spent forty years on the backside of the desert before leading Israel.

God used silence to train his spirit and solitude to shape his humility.

What looked like a demotion was development.

Many young people quit when reward is delayed, but mentors teach them to stay steady under strain.

Growth doesn't come from escape—it comes from endurance.

Pressure is not proof that God left you; it's evidence that He trusts you with weight.

When God brings you out of hiding, He brings you into responsibility—because revelation is always followed by assignment.

From Pain to Purpose

Look back and trace the pattern.

Every detour carried direction. Every setback taught strength.

What felt wasted was actually rehearsal for where you are now.

- **Joseph wasn't betrayed**—he was sent.

- **Ruth wasn't abandoned**—she was aligned.

- **Paul wasn't blocked**—he was blessed.

- **David wasn't hiding**—he was being honed.

God never wastes a wound.

Your pain is a prophecy in disguise.

And one day, the same story that once broke you will build someone else.

Reflective Questions:

1. Can you recall a moment when God's "No" turned out to protect you?

2. What lessons have your delays and disappointments taught you about trust?

3. How has pressure revealed what was truly in your heart?

4. Who has God used as a living example of purpose under pressure in your life?

5. How might your current detour be preparing you to mentor others?

Reflective Summary:

God's redirection is mentorship in motion.

He trains you through transitions and strengthens you through setbacks.

When you surrender to His hand, even pain becomes purposeful.

Rejection refines you.

Pressure produces you.

And every closed door becomes a classroom of destiny.

You are not lost—you are being positioned for purpose.

Prayer for Divine Redirection and Purpose:

Heavenly Father,

Thank You for ordering my steps even when I don't understand the path.

When doors close and plans change, teach me to trust Your timing.

Help me see that pressure is preparation and redirection is protection.

Surround me with mentors who model faith under fire. Strengthen my heart to endure until Your purpose is revealed.

And when You bring me into my assignment, let me use every lesson to lift others.

In Jesus' name, Amen.

Chapter 6 – Mentored by the Mission: Walking Out the Assignment Through Service

"And whosoever will be chief among you, let him be your servant."

— **Matthew 20:27 (KJV)**

Purpose Begins With Serving

Many people want to discover their purpose but forget that purpose is revealed through service.

God often mentors us through the very missions He assigns. Every time you *help, give, or listen,* you're not just meeting a need—you're being shaped by God.

Dr. Martin Luther King Jr. once said, *"Everybody can be great, because everybody can serve."*

Greatness in God's kingdom isn't about position; it's about participation.

Service is the classroom where *obedience, compassion, and humility* are taught.

When you serve, God teaches you who you are becoming. Purpose doesn't begin on a platform; it begins at the doorstep of service.

Mentorship Through Service

Some people enter your life by assignment, not accident. They are heaven's instruments to unlock something within you.

Helping them becomes part of your own development.

Serving trains the heart *to listen, to care, and to discern.* It removes selfish ambition and replaces it with compassion.

It teaches you to recognize the voice of the Holy Ghost in everyday encounters.

Dr. James Dobson once wrote, *"Children are not casual guests in our home; they have been loaned to us temporarily for the purpose of loving them."*

That principle extends beyond parenting—it describes all spiritual mentorship.

The people God places around you are loans of heaven, temporary trusts meant to shape both you and them.

The Rich Man and Lazarus: The Missed Mission

In **Luke 16,** Jesus tells of a rich man living in luxury while poor **Lazarus** lay outside his gate.

The rich man's sin wasn't wealth—it was **blindness.** His mission sat at his doorstep, but comfort made him careless.

Lazarus represented purpose in disguise.

Likewise, God may position someone near you who seems insignificant, but your response determines how much more He can trust you with.

If you ignore your Lazarus, you risk missing your lesson.

Elijah and the Widow: Learning Obedience Through Service

When **Elijah** met the **widow of Zarephath (1 Kings 17),** both were desperate—one for food, the other for faith.

God used service to mentor them both. Elijah learned **trust;** the widow learned **obedience.**

Her small act of giving her last meal released abundance.

Sometimes the miracle isn't in what you have—
it's in what you're willing to give.

The kitchen became their classroom; the meal
became their miracle.

Every act of obedience, however small, is divine
mentorship in motion.

Learning by Doing

Many young people wait until they *"get it together"* before serving, but service is how God gets you together.

- **Moses** learned leadership in the wilderness.

- **David** learned courage in the pasture.

- **The disciples** learned faith by feeding crowds and facing storms.

God doesn't wait for perfection; He perfects you while you serve.

Every *volunteer* moment, every act of *compassion*, every *mentoring conversation* trains your spirit for greater responsibility.

Walking Out the Assignment

Promotion is not the finish line—it's the beginning of stewardship.

When God opens a door, He watches how you walk through it.

- **Joseph** didn't relax in Pharaoh's palace; he managed a famine with integrity.

- **Daniel** didn't compromise in Babylon; he stayed faithful in prayer.

Success tests faithfulness. Purpose isn't proven by applause but by consistency.

Do the unseen things well—*pray, study, show up, serve*—and God will trust you with what others can see.

Stewardship of People

Your assignment will always include people.

You're not merely managing duties; you're shepherding hearts.

Mentorship means *showing up, listening without judgment, and correcting with love.*

As **Dr. Dobson** taught, *"The goal is to shape the will without breaking the spirit."*

That's how Jesus trained His disciples—with *truth, tenderness, and time.*

The same principle mentors' *children, coworkers, or church members today.*

A Lesson in Compassion: Mentored by the Mission

There was a time, back in the winter of 2003, when I was asked to drive my niece to school. She had missed her bus, and as her uncle, I felt it was my duty to help her.

Little did I know that it was a set-up by God.

While driving through the cold streets of Cleveland, I noticed a man, in the middle of the street begging for help as cars sped past.

He looked desperate and invisible to everyone around him as he moved from one vehicle to the next.

As he approached my vehicle asking for rent money, I gently waved him off to protect my niece.

Then the Lord spoke:

"Whoso stoppeth his ears at the cry of the poor, he also shall cry himself, but shall not be heard."

(Proverbs 21:13)

I froze. I knew God was talking to me.

I called the man back, gave him what I had, and promised to return. Over the next several months I paid his rent, bought him food, clothes, and simply listened.

I didn't realize it, but God was mentoring me through that mission—teaching me to see people, not problems.

Compassion became my classroom.

Later, after losing my job, the Lord surprised me with a $26,000 blessing.

That miracle wasn't random—it was God rewarding obedience.

He had taught me that compassion always precedes promotion.

Purpose Under Pressure

Pressure is the test of purpose.

Behavioral psychologist B. F. Skinner showed that **consistent reinforcement builds strength;**

Scripture says the same:

"No chastening for the present seemeth joyous… nevertheless afterward it yieldeth the peaceable fruit of righteousness." **(Hebrews 12:11)**

Endurance under pressure proves readiness.

Like **David** in his cave or **Joseph** in his prison, your private faithfulness prepares you for public **responsibility.**

When God brings you out of hiding, He brings you into responsibility—because revelation is always followed by assignment.

The Heart of the Mission

God never wastes encounters.

Every person He places in your path is a lesson in love.

When you serve, you're learning *humility, patience, and trust.*

The mission shapes your motives until service becomes second nature.

You don't need a title to have a ministry—you just need a towel.

Jesus proved that when He washed His disciples' feet.

When you serve, you are mentored by the Master Himself.

Reflective Questions:

1. Who has God placed in your life to serve or mentor right now?

2. What "Lazarus" might be waiting at your gate, unnoticed?

3. How has serving others changed your view of success?

4. What small act of obedience could unlock a miracle today?

5. Who is watching your example and learning from your faithfulness?

Reflective Summary:

We are all called to serve, and through service, God mentors us into maturity.

The mission is not about status—it's about shaping.

Every act of obedience is a lesson; every encounter a classroom.

You don't need a pulpit to preach; your life is the sermon.

As you serve, you'll discover that ministry isn't about doing for God but becoming like Him.

And in time, you'll realize that you were not only helping others—you were being mentored by the mission.

Prayer for a Servant's Heart:

Heavenly Father,

Thank You for trusting me with people, not just positions. Teach me to see every person as a divine assignment, not an interruption.

Give me a heart to serve with humility and joy.

When I grow weary, remind me that service is how You shape me. When I serve others, remind me that I'm serving You.

Use my hands to help, my heart to heal, and my words to build.

Mentor me through every mission You send—and let my life reflect Your glory.

In Jesus' name, Amen.

Chapter 7 – Staying the Course

How Perseverance Turns Mentorship into Maturity

"For ye have need of patience, that, after ye have done the will of God, ye might receive the promise."

— Hebrews 10:36 (KJV)

Introduction – When the Lesson Becomes the Test

There comes a time in every believer's life when the journey itself becomes the classroom. You've heard God's promises, endured His correction, and now you find yourself standing between what you expected and what you're experiencing.

That space is where perseverance is born. It's where the mentored become mature.

Every lesson God teaches must eventually be tested. The question is not whether you've learned something—it's whether you'll stay the course when the process grows long, quiet, and uncomfortable.

The writer of **Hebrews** reminds us, *"For ye have need of patience, that, after ye have done the will of God, ye might receive the promise."*

In other words, faith is not just about starting strong; it's about finishing well.

Dr. James Dobson, the founder of Focus on the Family, once said, *"Faith grows best in the soil of adversity."* God doesn't use comfort to confirm your calling—He uses challenge to develop your character.

When you remain faithful through pressure, you graduate from simply knowing truth to living truth. That's how God mentors' endurance.

1. Mentorship Beyond the Moment

It's easy to listen to a mentor when the lessons feel exciting, but true growth happens when the instruction feels heavy.

Every athlete knows that muscles grow by resistance. Likewise, the spirit grows by staying under divine tension.

Erik Erikson, a renowned developmental psychologist, described growth as a series of crises—moments of testing that form identity. Each challenge, he said, *is "a turning point where development can move forward or backward."*

Spiritually speaking, God allows those same turning points in our lives. Each hardship becomes a chance to either lean into His guidance or walk away from His correction.

The difference between a believer who matures and one who quits is not intelligence, charisma, or talent—*it's consistency*. Staying the course when you feel unseen is what separates a seed from a tree.

2. The Science of Staying Steady

Modern psychology calls this *resilience*—the ability to bounce back after difficulty.

Dr. Viktor Frankl, a Holocaust survivor and psychiatrist, wrote that *"those who have a 'why' to live can bear almost any 'how.'"*

When faith gives you a why, you can endure almost any how.

Resilience isn't denial; it's perspective. It's seeing God's hand in seasons that make no sense. It's believing that pain can have purpose and that even the detours are part of divine direction.

Jean Piaget, another great developmental theorist, taught that growth happens through stages of adaptation. Each stage builds upon the last.

God does the same with our faith—He builds us layer by layer. Each test adds structure to what He's already begun in us.

You may not feel stronger right now, but every trial is reinforcing the foundation of your destiny.

3. Joseph: The Mentored Survivor

Joseph's story isn't only about betrayal—it's about consistency under pressure.

When his brothers threw him into the pit, when Potiphar's wife falsely accused him, and when the butler forgot him, Joseph kept doing the one thing most people neglect: **he remained faithful.**

That's what staying the course looks like.

Every season became a mentoring classroom—teaching Joseph how to *think, act, and respond like a leader.* Before he could manage Egypt's abundance, he had to learn how to manage adversity with grace.

Psychologists call this **adaptive behavior**—the ability to adjust your response to life's challenges.

Spiritually, we call it **sanctification**—the process by which God refines the heart.

What makes **Joseph** remarkable is not just his dream, but his *discipline*. He didn't allow injustice to make him bitter. His *perseverance* prepared him for purpose.

4. The Role of Mentorship in Emotional Growth

Dr. Urie Bronfenbrenner, a pioneer in developmental psychology, said, *"Every child needs at least one adult who is irrationally crazy about them."*

That truth mirrors God's heart in mentorship. Every young believer needs someone who refuses to give up on them—someone who keeps believing, even when they stumble.

For the mentoree, that constancy becomes stability. **For the mentor,** it becomes obedience.

When young people are surrounded by inconsistent voices, the mentor becomes their anchor. God uses mentorship to build **emotional resilience**—*the capacity to trust again, to hope again, and to continue even when others give up.*

That's why **Paul** said, *"Be ye followers of me, even as I also am of Christ."* **(1 Corinthians 11:1).** Mentorship is not about control—it's about **example**. It's the bridge between *instruction and imitation.*

5. The Psychology of Endurance

Behavioral specialist B.F. Skinner taught that reinforcement—**positive or negative**—shapes future behavior.

In God's system, *obedience i*s its own reinforcement. Every time you obey through pain, God strengthens the pattern of faith inside you.

In the world's system, people need applause to stay motivated.

In God's system, the Holy Ghost becomes your encouragement—whispering, *"Keep going. I'm with you."*

Each step of obedience rewires your response to hardship. You stop panicking and start praising. You stop resisting correction and start embracing growth.

That's divine conditioning—the Spirit shaping your reflexes until perseverance becomes your natural response.

6. Jesus: The Perfect Example of Endurance

No one modeled perseverance better than Jesus.

In Gethsemane, He prayed through the pain. On the cross, He forgave through the suffering. In death, He trusted through the silence.

Hebrews 12:2 tells us, *"Looking unto Jesus... who for the joy that was set before him endured the cross, despising the shame."*

The cross was the greatest mentoring moment in human history. Through suffering, Jesus showed us how to stay the course—not by striving, but by surrendering. Pain became the pulpit from which He preached obedience.

7. When the Student Becomes the Example

Maturity is not just surviving storms—it's learning to guide others through theirs.

Albert Bandura, the father of social learning theory, taught that people don't just learn by being told; they learn by watching others.

That's how spiritual mentoring works. *Someone is watching you—your reactions, your faith, your perseverance.* Without even realizing it, your endurance is mentoring someone else.

You may not have a title, but your example is a sermon. Staying faithful when it's hardest is what inspires others to believe they can do the same.

8. Staying the Course When It's Hard to See

There will be seasons when the reward seems far away—when the mentoring feels thankless and the mission feels heavy.

During those times, remember this truth: the mentor's peace comes from **obedience,** not outcomes.

God doesn't measure success by speed, but by stamina. He is more pleased by your endurance than your excitement.

When you stay the course, you mirror His consistency. And that consistency becomes your crown.

Reflective Questions:

1. What area of your life is testing your patience and perseverance right now?

2. How has God used previous endurance to strengthen your present faith?

3. Who might be watching your example of steadfastness and learning from it?

4. How does understanding emotional and spiritual growth help you interpret hardship differently?

5. What spiritual habits can you develop to help you stay the course when life gets difficult?

Reflective Summary:

Staying the course is more than patience—it's partnership with God.

He mentors us through time, through tension, and through testing until we reflect the image of His Son.

- **Every delay** strengthens discipline.
- **Every hardship** deepens humility.
- **Every challenge** builds character.

When you look back, you'll realize God was never distant—He was deliberate.

You are not just surviving; you are becoming.

The storm was never meant to sink you—it was meant to strengthen you.

Stay the course. Your consistency is your crown.

Prayer for Endurance and Maturity:

Heavenly Father,

Thank You for being faithful when I grow weary. Teach me to trust Your timing when the road is long and uncertain.

Give me strength to endure what I don't understand, and wisdom to see purpose in every delay.

Help me stay steady under pressure, humble under blessing, and hopeful under trial.

Let my perseverance become an example to others, and let my life reflect Your glory.

When my race is finished, let me say with confidence, "I have kept the faith."

In Jesus' name, Amen.

Chapter 8 – From Mentee to Mentor: Passing On What Life Taught You

How Emotional Wholeness Produces Spiritual Leadership

"And the things that thou hast heard of me among many witnesses, the same commit thou to faithful men, who shall be able to teach others also."

— 2 Timothy 2:2 (KJV)

Introduction – The Journey Comes Full Circle

There comes a time in every believer's walk when the lessons of yesterday become the instructions for someone else's tomorrow.

You've prayed, endured, learned, and matured—not just for yourself, but for those God will send behind you.

Paul told **Timothy,** *"The things that thou hast heard of me… commit thou to faithful men."*

That's how the Kingdom grows—one life mentoring another, one testimony becoming another's training ground.

When you've been through the fire and refused to quit, your life becomes a living classroom. You no longer speak from theory; you speak from transformation.

1. Mentorship as Maturity

True maturity is not just measured by how much you know, but by how much you can give away.

The mentee becomes a mentor not when they've achieved perfection, but when they've learned humility through experience.

The same pain that once puzzled you now becomes your platform to teach.

The same confusion that once broke you now equips you to guide others through their storms.

This is how God works—He turns students into stewards.

You are not just a product of what you've been taught; you are now a vessel of what you've learned through living.

2. Freud: The Struggle Within

The early psychologist **Sigmund Freud** believed that every person lives in tension between three inner voices: **the id** (our impulses), **the ego** (our reason), and **the superego** (our moral conscience).

Though Freud wrote in clinical terms, his insight aligns with Scripture.

The Apostle Paul said, *"The good that I would I do not: but the evil which I would not, that I do."*

(Romans 7:19)

That's the same inner conflict Freud described—what we call the battle between **the flesh** and **the spirit.**

But here's where divine mentorship surpasses psychology:

What Freud called the "superego," the believer calls **the Holy Ghost.**

He doesn't just restrain behavior; He renews the heart.

He transforms desire itself.

Without spiritual mentoring and accountability, people remain trapped between impulse and intention—always wanting better but never becoming better.

Godly mentors help bridge that gap. They teach us how to bring *emotion, faith, and decision* under the control of the Spirit.

3. Erik Erikson: The Stages of Becoming

Freud showed the struggle. **Erik Erikson** showed the stages through which people grow.

He taught that life unfolds in seasons—each one presenting a challenge that either builds or breaks character.

For instance: **Infants** learn *trust versus mistrust.*

Adolescents struggle with *identity versus confusion.*

Adults wrestle with *purpose versus stagnation.*

Erikson's theory mirrors spiritual development. Each stage requires guidance—someone who models what faith looks like in real life.

That's why mentorship is so vital in the Church.

Without godly examples, people get stuck spiritually where they got stuck emotionally.

A young believer may know Scripture but still lack *stability* because no one helped them translate knowledge into life practice.

Mentorship bridges that gap. It teaches believers not just what to believe, but how to become.

When **Paul** told the Corinthians, *"Ye have ten thousand instructors in Christ, but not many fathers,"* **(1 Corinthians 4:15)** he was describing what Erikson called *identity crisis.*

People can have teachers, but if they never have fathers or mothers in the faith, they struggle to mature emotionally and spiritually.

4. Carl Jung: The Journey to Wholeness

Carl Jung, one of Freud's early students, went further. He said that growth requires confronting the shadow—the hidden parts of ourselves we'd rather deny.

Jung's words echo a biblical truth: you cannot heal what you refuse to face.

The Holy Ghost serves as the divine Counselor, shining light on the areas we hide from others—and even from ourselves.

When you allow God to deal with the shadow, He doesn't shame you; He shapes you.

He uses truth to deliver, not destroy.

Jung wrote, *"Until you make the unconscious conscious, it will direct your life and you will call it fate."*

That's what happens when people avoid spiritual mentorship. They live in cycles, calling it **"bad luck,"** when in truth, it's unhealed patterns.

God sends mentors—pastors, parents, teachers, or elders—to help bring the unconscious to the surface, to help us see what we've ignored, and to train us to walk in awareness and freedom.

5. The Holy Ghost: The Master Mentor

Freud analyzed the mind. Erikson mapped development. Jung explored the soul.

But the **Holy Ghost** perfects them all.

He is the Master Mentor—guiding, correcting, and empowering us beyond human ability.

Jesus called Him *"the Spirit of truth"* who would *"guide you into all truth."* **(John 16:13)**

Human mentorship helps shape character, but divine mentorship transforms nature.

A mentor can challenge you, but only the Spirit can change you.

Every Christian mentor must therefore stay submitted to the Spirit's leading. Otherwise, they risk teaching others their own opinions instead of God's principles.

6. Becoming the Mentor You Needed

There's a saying: *"Be the person you needed when you were younger."*

That's what spiritual maturity looks like.

You might not have had perfect parents, pastors, or examples—but through **the Holy Ghost,** you can become the one God uses to fill that gap for someone else.

When you mentor others, you multiply what God has done in you.

Your words may plant the seed, but your consistency waters it.

Mentorship is not about position—it's about presence.

It's *showing up, listening, guiding,* and *loving* until the mentee learns to stand on their own.

The world doesn't just need more preachers—it needs more **fathers** and **mothers** in the faith who live what they preach.

7. Lessons from Life's Classroom

By this stage of life, you've learned that some of your greatest teachers never stood in a pulpit.

They were the seasons, struggles, and silent moments where God Himself instructed you.

Now He asks you to take those lessons and invest them in others.

Your story carries credibility. Your scars carry wisdom.

Don't hide them—use them.

Remember: **Moses** mentored Joshua. **Naomi** mentored Ruth. **Elijah** mentored Elisha. **Paul** mentored Timothy.

And Jesus mentored twelve men who would one day change the world.

Each of them passed on what life—and the Spirit—taught them.

Now it's your turn.

8. Mentorship as Legacy

When you pour into others, you build something time can't erase.

You may never see your name on a marquee, but your influence will live in the lives you shaped.

God measures legacy not by how long you lived, but by how many lives you lifted.

Every act of mentorship—*every prayer, every correction, every word of encouragement*—creates ripples that will outlast your lifetime.

This is what it means to walk in purpose: You become a vessel through which God passes *wisdom, compassion, and strength* to the next generation.

Reflective Questions:

1. Who has God used to mentor you through key stages of your life and faith?

2. What lessons from your own growth can help someone else avoid unnecessary pain?

3. How can you integrate prayer and psychological awareness when mentoring others?

4. Are there "shadow areas" in your life that God may be asking you to confront before you lead others?

5. Who in your life is waiting for you to say, "Come, walk with me"?

Reflective Summary:

Spiritual mentorship is not a position—it's a progression.

You begin as a student of pain, become a steward of purpose, and end as a servant who pours out wisdom.

Freud showed the conflict. Erikson showed the stages. Jung showed the shadow.

But the Holy Ghost shows the way—leading us from brokenness to **balance**, from confusion to **clarity**, from learning to **leading.**

When you embrace this call, your life becomes a seed that multiplies beyond your years.

You no longer just survive the lessons—you embody them.

And through you, the next generation learns that purpose is not a destination; it's a legacy of mentorship and maturity.

Prayer for Spiritual Maturity and Mentorship:

Heavenly Father,

Thank You for every mentor You've sent to guide me, and for the grace that turned my pain into purpose.

Teach me to *lead with humility and love, to listen before I speak, and to see others through Your eyes.*

Reveal the areas in me that still need refining, and give me courage to confront them with truth and grace.

Fill me with Your Spirit, that I may mentor others not from pride, but from compassion.

Let my life be an example of Your patience, power, and peace.

And may every word I speak and every soul I reach bring glory to Your name.

In Jesus' name, Amen.

Chapter 9 – Passing the Baton: Training the Next Generation of Believers

Raising Disciples Who Will Carry the Fire Forward

"And the things that thou hast heard of me among many witnesses, the same commit thou to faithful men, who shall be able to teach others also."

— 2 Timothy 2:2 (KJV)

Introduction – The Baton Must Be Passed

Every race has a moment when one runner must hand the baton to another.

If the exchange is mishandled, the entire team suffers—even if every runner was fast.

That's where the Church is today. One generation has run with *faith, fire, and endurance*—but unless we intentionally train and trust the next generation, the race will stall.

The Apostle Paul understood this well. That's why he told Timothy, *"Commit these truths to faithful men."*

He was saying, "Don't let what God taught you stop with you."

True mentorship doesn't end when the student succeeds—it continues when the student starts sowing.

1. The Mandate to Reproduce

The Great Commission was never just about conversion—it was about continuation.

Jesus didn't just make disciples; He trained disciple-makers.

God's plan for sustaining the Church has always been generational.

He calls every mature believer to be a link in the chain of legacy.

- When **Moses**' time ended, **Joshua** was ready.

- When **Elijah** departed, **Elisha** picked up the mantle.

- When **Paul** was imprisoned, **Timothy** carried on the mission.

Each generation of believers carries both a *responsibility* and a *revelation:*

"I must not let the flame die with me."

You may not stand behind a pulpit, but you still have a platform—*your home, your job, your community.* Every word of faith you speak, every act of love you show, becomes part of God's ongoing story.

2. The Psychology of Imitation and Influence

Developmental psychologist **Albert Bandura,** known for his Social Learning Theory, taught that most learning happens not through instruction but through imitation.

People don't just listen to what they're told—they become what they see.

That's why Jesus didn't simply preach the Gospel; He modeled it.

He said, *"I have given you an example, that ye should do as I have done to you."* **(John 13:15)**

When young believers watch how we *pray, forgive, handle conflict, or walk through storms,* they're taking mental notes. Our reactions mentor them more deeply than our words.

Bandura's research confirms what Scripture already revealed:

"Be ye followers of me, even as I also am of Christ." — **1 Corinthians 11:1**

The next generation will not be shaped by our sermons alone, but by *our consistency—our ability to live what we proclaim.*

3. Dr. James Dobson: Building Faith in the Home

Dr. James Dobson, the Christian psychologist and founder of Focus on the Family, often said, *"The most important work you will ever do will be within the walls of your own home."*

Mentorship begins with relationship—and no relationship is more formative than family.

When children grow up watching faith in action—*prayer before meals, forgiveness after arguments, and worship in hard times*—they **internalize God's reality** long before they understand doctrine.

Dobson observed that spiritual consistency in the home produces *emotional stability* in children.

It's not perfection that shapes them—it's presence.

Your willingness to model *repentance, humility, and faith* teaches them how to walk with God long after you're gone.

If the home is healthy, the next generation will carry faith into the culture.

4. Training Through Trust

One of the hardest parts of mentorship is knowing when to release those you've trained.

Many mentors struggle with letting go, fearing that the next generation isn't ready.

But Jesus Himself trusted the disciples with the Gospel, knowing full well they would make mistakes. He said, *"Greater works shall ye do."* **(John 14:12)**

He didn't just prepare them for ministry—He believed in them.

Likewise, mentors must learn to trust the God who worked through them to now work through others.

Your mentee may stumble, but if they've seen your faith, they'll find their footing again.

Mentorship that doesn't end in release becomes control.

Mentorship that ends in empowerment becomes legacy.

5. Mentorship Beyond the Church Walls

The next generation won't all find their calling in the pulpit—but they will find it in *the classroom, the workplace, the military, and the marketplace.*

That's why mentorship must move beyond church pews and into everyday life.

- A teacher can mentor through patience.
- A business owner can mentor through integrity.

- A coach can mentor through encouragement.
- A father can mentor through example.

Your faith doesn't stop at the sanctuary—it walks with you into society.

As **Dr. Martin Luther King Jr.** said, *"Life's most persistent and urgent question is, 'What are you doing for others?'"*

Every believer is called to model righteousness where darkness reigns. That's how nations are changed—one mentored life at a time.

6. Avoiding the Generational Gap

One of the enemy's greatest tactics is to divide generations.

- **Older believers** say, "The young people don't listen."

- **Younger believers** say, "The older folks don't understand."

But Scripture bridges that gap:

"One generation shall praise thy works to another, and shall declare thy mighty acts."

— Psalm 145:4

Unity doesn't mean uniformity. The young bring energy; the old bring experience. Together, they carry endurance.

When the Church learns to walk in intergenerational partnership, revival becomes sustainable.

We must stop criticizing the next generation long enough to start coaching them.

7. The Model of Jesus and His Disciples

Jesus didn't just teach His disciples—He walked with them daily.

They watched Him *pray in Gethsemane, serve the poor, and love His enemies.*

He corrected them gently when they misunderstood, and He celebrated them when they obeyed.

Even when **Peter** denied Him, Jesus restored him with purpose: *"Feed My sheep."*

That's what mentorship looks like—truth and grace working together.

Jesus' model shows us that the goal of mentorship isn't control, but cultivation.

When you mentor someone in love, you help them discover their calling and empower them to carry it further than you did.

8. Preparing for the Handoff

In relay races, the most critical moment isn't how fast you run—it's how smoothly you pass the baton.

You can't hand off what you haven't carried.

And you can't impart what you haven't lived.

Before you pass the baton, make sure your mentees have seen your *faith tested and proven.* Let them see you *pray through pain, forgive offenses, and keep believing when things fall apart.*

They don't need perfect mentors—they need present ones.

Once they see what endurance looks like, they'll know how to run when it's their turn.

9. A Closed Hand Can't Receive

One of the greatest barriers to effective mentorship is stinginess of spirit.

Some people want the benefits of community without the burden of contribution.

They're quick to take but slow to give; eager to be helped but unwilling to help.

But Scripture warns, *"There is that scattereth, and yet increaseth; and there is that withholdeth more than is meet, but it tendeth to poverty."*

— **Proverbs 11:24 (KJV)**

A closed hand cannot give—and it also cannot receive.

God designed giving as the circulatory system of His Kingdom.

When you bless others, He keeps the supply flowing.

When you hoard, you clog the pipeline of provision.

Even modern psychology confirms this truth. **Dr. Martin Seligman,** one of the founders of Positive Psychology, discovered that acts of *generosity* reduce *anxiety* and *increase life satisfaction.*

The human spirit was made to give—because we were created in the image of a generous God.

Those who withhold find themselves isolated and anxious. They drain relationships because they approach every interaction with the question, *"What can I get?"* instead of *"What can I give?"*

But those who share—time, money, wisdom, encouragement—become magnets for God's favor.

Jesus said,

"Give, and it shall be given unto you; good measure, pressed down, and shaken together, and running over."

— Luke 6:38

True mentors live with open hands.

They understand that what you release multiplies, and what you hoard diminishes.

Every resource you share—whether financial, emotional, or spiritual—is a seed that guarantees future harvest.

If you want your life to overflow, start pouring into others.

10. Reflection – The Baton Is in Your Hand

Every believer stands somewhere in the relay of faith.

Some are just beginning to run. Others are catching their breath. And some are now holding the baton, ready to pass it on.

Wherever you stand, remember: *Faith is not meant to die in your generation.*

You are part of God's generational plan—one link in the eternal chain of mentorship.

Train others. Encourage the young. Speak life into the discouraged.

Because when you pass the baton well, you ensure the race never ends.

Reflective Questions:

1. Who handed you the baton of faith, and how did their example shape you?

2. What practical ways can you mentor or disciple someone in your sphere of influence?

3. Have you modeled enough faith and consistency for others to follow?

4. Are there areas where you need to release control and trust God with those you've trained?

5. What specific legacy of faith do you want to leave behind for the next generation?

Reflective Summary:

Mentorship is not just about knowledge—it's about continuation.

The same God who trained Moses to lead Israel and Timothy to shepherd the Church is calling you to carry—and pass—the flame.

Faith is generational, and every generation has a responsibility to the one that follows.

When you model Christ, speak truth, and serve in love, you hand off something eternal.

Don't drop the baton. Don't let the race end with you.

Keep running, keep teaching, and keep trusting that the next generation will do greater works than you ever imagined.

Prayer for Legacy and Leadership:

Heavenly Father,

Thank You for the mentors who poured into my life, and for the opportunity to pour into others.

Help me to pass the baton of faith with wisdom and grace.

Teach me to see the potential in others, to encourage them when they stumble, and to release them when it's time to run.

May my words inspire, my actions instruct, and my love restore. Let my legacy not be titles or trophies, but transformed lives that glorify You.

And may the flame of faith never go out in my generation.

In Jesus' name, Amen.

Chapter 10 – The Mentor's Reward: Seeing Fruit from Faithfulness

When Obedience Becomes Legacy

"His lord said unto him, Well done, thou good and faithful servant: thou hast been faithful over a few things, I will make thee ruler over many things: enter thou into the joy of thy lord."

— Matthew 25:21 (KJV)

Introduction – The Reward Is in the Faithfulness

In a world obsessed with recognition, God measures success by faithfulness.

You may never stand on a stage, but if you've been consistent in pouring into others, heaven takes notice.

Every seed of love, every word of encouragement, every act of service is recorded in eternity.

Some rewards are visible now—*changed lives, restored families, renewed faith.* Others remain hidden until the day when God Himself says, *"Well done, good and faithful servant."*

Faithfulness is its own reward because it proves your heart belongs to the One who called you.

1. Sowing in Tears, Reaping in Joy

Many mentors labor without applause. They *pray, teach, give, and correct*—often wondering if their efforts matter.

But Scripture promises:

"They that sow in tears shall reap in joy."

— **Psalm 126:5**

Sometimes the seeds you plant don't sprout immediately. The young person you mentor may wander. The person you invested in may fall short. But don't lose heart.

The same God who sent you to sow will send the rain to make it grow.

Mentorship is not about instant results—it's about eternal returns.

Every seed sown in faith produces fruit in God's timing.

2. The Spiritual Return on Investment

Jesus told a story in **Matthew 25** about servants who were each given a measure of resources.

Two of them multiplied what they were given; one buried his talent in fear.

The lesson is simple: God rewards stewardship, not stagnation.

He doesn't ask for perfection—He asks for participation.

When you mentor someone, you are multiplying the Kingdom's investment.

Every time you *teach, guide, or encourage*, you increase heaven's return.

Faithful mentors will hear the same commendation as those who expanded their talents:

"Well done, thou good and faithful servant: thou hast been faithful over a few things, I will make thee ruler over many things."

— Matthew 25:21

In God's economy, what you pour into others never leaves your life—it comes back multiplied in ways you can't predict.

3. The Invisible Harvest

Some of the most powerful rewards in life are invisible.

You may never see the full impact of your mentoring on earth—but that doesn't mean it wasn't fruitful.

- **Consider Moses**: he never entered the Promised Land, yet his faith shaped **Joshua,** who led a nation across the Jordan.

- **Consider Barnabas:** he trained Saul of Tarsus, who became **the Apostle Paul.**

Your influence may live on in someone you once encouraged and forgot about.

One conversation, one prayer, one small act of guidance can ripple through generations.

As **Dr. Henry Cloud**, Christian psychologist and author of Boundaries, once said:

"Your greatest fruit often grows on someone else's tree."

That is the mentor's reward—knowing that God can use your life to produce harvests you'll never personally harvest, but heaven will credit to your account.

When God Mentors the Mentor

Before I could ever mentor others, God Himself had to mentor me.

My earliest lesson came long before I knew what *"discipleship"* meant. I was just a boy in the fifth or sixth grade—*angry, jealous,* and *lost.* A friend had things I didn't, and in my foolishness, I broke into his home and stole fourteen dollars.

At the time, it seemed small, but guilt followed me like a shadow. I couldn't eat, couldn't sleep, and finally confessed.

What I didn't understand then was that I was already in class—God's classroom. He was teaching me *repentance* before I even knew the word.

That day, I learned that sin may promise excitement, but it always pays with shame. Though I was too young to understand theology, I somehow knew I had to make it right.

Without anyone telling me, I repaid the boy double what I had taken. Later in life, I would read in **Exodus 22** that restitution was God's standard. The Spirit had already written that law on my heart.

That was divine mentorship—God *correcting, guiding, and shaping* me long before I ever stood behind a pulpit. Before I could guide others, He guided me. Before I could teach *repentance,* He taught it to me through conviction and mercy.

4. Peace After Planting

After years of laboring, mentoring, and giving, every faithful servant must learn the art of rest.

Faithfulness is not frantic—*it's consistent.*

You do what God asks, and then you trust Him with the results.

Some mentors struggle with releasing those they've trained. But if you've *poured out truth, modeled integrity, and prayed faithfully,* you've done your part. The rest belongs to God.

Jesus modeled this when He prayed,

"I have finished the work which Thou gavest Me to do."

— John 17:4

He didn't say He had fixed everyone or convinced everyone—He said He had finished His assignment.

That's what true mentors do: *they complete the mission God gave them and rest in His promise of reward.*

Personal Reflection – The Fruit of Faithfulness

When I look back over my life, I can trace the thread of divine mentorship through every season.

God mentored me through conviction as a child, through trials in the military, through seasons of isolation in Hawaii, and through restoration after a failed marriage to Jo.

Each season was both correction and preparation. God was not punishing me—He was training me.

Those lessons became the foundation for the way I now mentor others. *I teach what I've lived. I encourage others not from theory but from testimony.*

Today, I see the fruit. My youngest daughter and one of my granddaughters walk in a measure of faith and stability that I didn't have growing up.

I've mentored many young men—some incarcerated, some searching for direction, one right in my neighborhood without a father to guide him.

I try to be a steady example, praying that something I say or do will plant hope in his heart and shape his future for the better.

I can't say everyone I've poured into has gone on to greatness. Some have drifted. Some may never return. But I've learned that the reward isn't in measurable results—it's in knowing I was faithful to obey God.

The mentor's peace comes from obedience, not outcomes.

5. The Joy of Multiplication

There is no greater joy than watching others grow into what you once prayed they'd become.

When a student becomes a teacher, when a child of faith becomes a soldier of Christ, when a once-broken life begins to bless others—that's the mentor's crown.

Paul said to the believers in Thessalonica,

"For what is our hope, or joy, or crown of rejoicing? Are not even ye in the presence of our Lord Jesus Christ at His coming?"

— 1 Thessalonians 2:19

Paul's reward wasn't money or fame—it was people.

The souls he had poured into were his eternal inheritance.

Your reward is not just in heaven—it's reflected every time someone you've helped stands strong in faith, saying, *"Because of your guidance, I didn't give up."*

That's when the tears make sense. That's when the sowing feels worth it.

6. The Promise of Overflow

God never forgets a giver. He never overlooks a mentor.

The same open-hand principle from Chapter 9 continues here: those who pour out will be poured into.

Proverbs 11:25 declares,

"The liberal soul shall be made fat: and he that watereth shall be watered also himself."

When you invest in others, heaven invests in you.

The more you give, the more grace God releases.

The more you bless, the more strength He restores.

This is not manipulation—**it's multiplication.**

When you refresh others, God refreshes you.

The mentor's reward is both **spiritual** and **emotional:** *peace, joy,* and *a sense of purpose* that no paycheck can buy.

7. Legacy Beyond a Lifetime

A faithful mentor never truly dies.

Their influence lives on in those they've touched.

Their prayers echo through generations.

Their teaching becomes someone else's compass in crisis. As long as truth remains alive in the heart of a student, the teacher still speaks.

Hebrews 11:4 reminds us,

"He being dead yet speaketh."

When you live a life worth imitating, your legacy becomes your loudest sermon.

You may leave this world someday, but your obedience will keep preaching.

Reflective Questions:

1. Who in your life reflects the seeds of faith you've planted?

2. What invisible fruit might be growing from your obedience?

3. Are you at peace with the work God called you to do, even if others don't notice?

4. How can you celebrate the victories of those you've mentored without needing credit?

5. What legacy of wisdom, generosity, or faithfulness do you want to leave behind?

Reflective Summary:

The mentor's reward is not fame—**it's fruit.**

It's the quiet joy of knowing that obedience bore eternal impact.

It's the peace of realizing that *every tear, every trial, every lesson you lived* became someone else's roadmap.

Faithful mentors don't compete—**they complete.**

They know that what they give away for God's glory multiplies far beyond their lifetime.

The harvest belongs to the Lord—but the joy belongs to those who sowed.

Prayer for the Faithful Servant:

Heavenly Father,

Thank You for the privilege of sowing into others. Even when I saw no fruit, You were working underground.

Teach me to trust Your timing and to rest in Your reward. Help me rejoice when others succeed and to celebrate the growth I may never see.

Let my faithfulness today become someone's foundation tomorrow.

And when my work is done, may I stand before You and hear the words every servant longs to hear:

"Well done, thou good and faithful servant."

In Jesus' name, Amen.

Chapter 11 – The Mantle And The Mission: Raising The Next Generation Of Mentors

"And it came to pass, when they were gone over, that Elijah said unto Elisha, Ask what I shall do for thee, before I be taken away from thee.

And Elisha said, I pray thee, let a double portion of thy spirit be upon me.

And he said, Thou hast asked a hard thing: nevertheless, if thou see me when I am taken from thee, it shall be so unto thee; but if not, it shall not be so."

— 2 Kings 2:9-10 (KJV)

When the Mantle Must Move Forward

Every generation comes to a crossing.

For Elijah and Elisha, it was the Jordan; for us, it is the line between memory and movement.

Elijah's season was ending; Elisha's was beginning.

But before Elijah could ascend, he turned and asked: *"What shall I do for thee, before I am taken away from thee?"*

That was not the inquiry of a man seeking praise, but of a mentor ready to release power.

Elisha's response revealed *hunger, humility*, and *holy ambition.*

He did not ask for comfort or applause. He asked for a double portion of his mentor's **spirit** — not twice Elijah's fame, but twice his faith.

The mantle would not fall on the casual or the complacent. It would rest only on those willing to *watch, wait,* and *walk close.*

So, it is today. Heaven is looking for Elishas who refuse to be spectators while their mentors ascend.

Every mantle requires movement. God never meant for *wisdom, anointing,* or *revelation* to die in the grave of the previous generation.

The fire that fell on Mount Carmel was never meant to go out—it was meant to spread.

The Mantle of Mentorship: Passing the Fire, Not Just the Title

When **Elijah** cast his mantle upon **Elisha** years earlier, he was not crowning him; he was calling him.

That mantle was a summons to service, a demand to leave the plow and pursue purpose.

True mentorship does not hand out crowns; it hands out crosses.

It does not promise comfort; it demands commitment.

It is less about titles and more about transformation.

A mentor's mantle is not a badge of status; it is a burden of service.

It means you will **pray** when others play, **stand** when others sit, and **weep over souls** while the world laughs at sin.

When **Elisha** asked for a double portion, he embraced the weight. The double portion brings double pressure and double responsibility.

Yet **Elisha** understood what many miss: the mantle doesn't represent ministry alone—it represents mission.

"One generation shall praise Thy works to another, and shall declare Thy mighty acts."

— Psalm 145:4

Mentorship is how God preserves fire through flesh. Every mantle must find a shoulder to rest upon.

The Multiplication Principle: From Mentee to Mentor

Paul told Timothy, *"The things that thou hast heard of me among many witnesses, the same commit thou to faithful men, who shall be able to teach others also."*

— 2 Timothy 2:2

That is the relay of faith—one generation teaching another until truth travels faster than the enemy's lies.

Mentorship is God's multiplication strategy.

It turns followers into leaders, servants into shepherds, and students into stewards.

The proof that you've been mentored well is not that you can quote your teacher but that you can continue their mission.

What God does in you is never complete until it continues through you.

When **Elisha** caught **Elijah's** mantle, he tore his old garments — you cannot wear the old and the new at once.

If you want the mantle of the future, you must release the garments of the past.

Modern Mantles: Mentorship Across Generations

"A coach will impact more people in one year than the average person will in an entire lifetime."

— **Billy Graham**

That statement captures spiritual multiplication: one faithful teacher, one invested life, can echo for decades. Graham didn't merely preach to the masses—he poured into men and women whose lives would outlast his own.

Rick Warren recalls how Billy Graham *"noticed"* him when he was a young pastor and mentored him for forty years. Through that relationship he learned not just to preach, but to *walk in humility, integrity,* and *purpose.*

Even Graham himself was shaped by mentors like **John Minder** of the Florida Bible Institute, who gave him his first opportunities to preach and affirmed his calling. Thus, the mantle moved from one obedient heart to another.

Pat Robertson likewise understood mentorship as the heartbeat of leadership. Through Regent University and the Christian Broadcasting Network, he focused on *"forging the next generation of servant-leaders."*

He taught that leadership without formation is fragile and that true success is measured by how well we prepare others to serve.

While **Graham** demonstrated the power of personal investment, **Robertson** built structures for ongoing *discipleship—schools, ministries, and broadcasts* designed to mentor through principle and practice.

Together they remind us that mentorship is not limited to a stage or a sermon; it is the quiet, consistent transfer of wisdom that turns students into stewards and followers into leaders.

We stand in their lineage—a line of those who saw potential in others and refused to let the mantle die with them.

Mentorship in an Age of Distraction

We live in a distracted world. Our youth are scrolling when they should be studying, comparing when they should be becoming.

Mentorship has been replaced by algorithms and discipleship by digital noise.

But God is calling us back to presence over platform. True mentorship cannot be downloaded; it must be demonstrated.

It's not measured by followers but by fruit.

The enemy's greatest weapon is noise. God is raising mentors who model stillness in a generation addicted to speed.

The next revival will not begin with a viral post but with a personal conversation.

Jesus built apprentices, not audiences. When He left, they didn't just remember His words—they reproduced His works.

The Wounded Mentor: Leading While Healing

Not every mentor starts whole. Some lead while *limping,* love while *bleeding,* teach *while still being taught.*

Peter knew that pain. After his denial, Jesus restored him and said, *"Feed My sheep."*

That's mentorship—healed people healing others.

Your scars qualify you. They prove you survived what someone else is still fighting.

You don't mentor from perfection but from proof.

The area of your greatest weakness often becomes your greatest wisdom.

Elijah once hid in a cave weary and afraid, yet God sent him back to anoint Elisha. Even in exhaustion, there was an assignment: Pass it on.

The Holy Ghost: The Master Mentor

Behind every true mentor stands the Holy Ghost—the Teacher who never sleeps. He guides into truth, convicts without condemning, and empowers without exhausting.

Human mentors can only point to the path; the Spirit walks it with you.

He turns experiences into *examples,* tests into *testimonies,* pain into *power.*

Without Him, mentorship is management; with Him, it is ministry.

Mentorship as Revival Strategy

Revival is not sustained by emotion but by impartation. Crowds may gather for a moment, but only mentorship builds movements.

Jesus mentored twelve who turned the world upside down.

When believers pour truth into others, fire spreads. When fathers and mothers nurture sons and daughters, nations shift.

The Church must return to relational revival— *teaching personally, correcting lovingly,* and *growing intentionally.*

That is how revival begins—not in noise but in nurture.

Finishing Faithful: Leaving the Mantle Behind

Elijah's greatest miracle was not the fire that fell—it was the man who followed.

Elisha proved that *Elijah's life was not in vain.*

Your legacy is not what you build but who you build.

When **Elisha** parted the Jordan with the mantle and cried, *"Where is the Lord God of Elijah?"* the waters obeyed.

Heaven confirmed that the torch had transferred.

Mentorship is complete when your mentees can *stand where you stood, fight where you fought, and win where you once wept.*

Don't let your anointing die with you. Find your **Elisha.** Pour until nothing is left, then watch the mantle fall.

Reflective Questions:

1. Who has carried a mantle that stirred you to pursue more of God?

2. What wisdom or gift is God calling you to pass on?

3. Who is watching your example and waiting for your guidance?

4. How has God turned your scars into strength for others?

5. What step will you take this week to mentor or disciple another life?

Reflective Summary:

The mantle is never meant to die with one generation. It moves from hand to hand, heart to heart, faith to faith.

Every **Elijah** needs an **Elisha,** and every **Elisha** must become one in turn.

Through mentorship, truth outlives trends and holiness outlasts hype.

We are the continuation of those who came before and the preparation for those who follow.

The Spirit still whispers: *"Pass it on."*

Teach. Train. Trust. And watch the mantle multiply again.

Closing Prayer – "Lord, Let the Mantle Fall"

Father, we thank You for Your faithfulness from generation to generation.

As Elijah passed his mantle to Elisha, let Your Spirit fall upon us today.

Awaken every mentor who has grown weary. Restore their passion to pour again.

Raise up fathers and mothers in the faith who will guide sons and daughters with wisdom and love.

Call forth the Elishas who wait in the fields—those who feel unseen and unprepared.

Clothe them with power. Let their eyes see Your movement and their hands carry Your fire.

Let every mantle of righteousness find a resting place. Let Your glory cover *homes, churches,* and *cities again.*

We say yes to the call, yes to the mission, yes to the mantle.

Closing Word

A Final Benediction from My Heart to Yours

I have lived long enough to see that the greatest rewards in life do not come from what we keep, but from what we give. Every act of obedience, every quiet prayer, and every seed sown in love is recorded in heaven's ledger.

I did not write this book to impress, but to impart — to tell someone who may feel *weary, forgotten, or overlooked* **that you were born for more.** You were born to love, to serve, to forgive, to rebuild, and to finish faithful.

If there is one truth that years of walking with God have taught me, it is this: the measure of a life is not in how high you climb, but in how faithfully you stand when no one applauds.

The world may never know your name, but if one soul finds hope because you kept going, then your living has not been in vain.

For as **Dr. Martin Luther King Jr**. reminded us,

"If I can help somebody as I pass along,

If I can cheer somebody with a word or song,

If I can show somebody he's traveling wrong,

Then my living shall not be in vain."

So, keep walking by faith. Keep serving with humility. Keep mentoring with love. Let your legacy be light.

When the journey grows long and your strength begins to fade, remember this promise:

"Be thou faithful unto death, and I will give thee a crown of life."

— Revelation 2:10 (KJV)

And when all is said and done, may the words of **the Apostle Paul** be true of you and me alike:

"I have fought a good fight, I have finished my course, I have kept the faith."

— 2 Timothy 4:7 (KJV)

Now unto Him who is able to keep you from falling, and to present you faultless before the presence of His glory with exceeding joy —

To the only wise God our Saviour, be glory and majesty, dominion and power, both now and forever. Amen.

(Jude 1:24–25)

— Eld Joel Latimore Jr.

Cleveland, Ohio – 2025

Acknowledgments

Every book is born through partnership — through the prayers, patience, and encouragement of people who believed long before the words were written.

I first give glory and thanks to **God the Father, Jesus Christ my Lord and Savior, and the Holy Ghost,** who continues to teach, comfort, and guide me daily. Without His grace, wisdom, and correction, these pages would be empty.

To every **mentor, pastor, and spiritual leader** who invested in me — thank you for modeling what it means to walk with integrity and humility before God. Your example laid the foundation upon which I now stand.

To the men and women, I have mentored through the years, and to those who have, in turn, mentored me — you are the living proof that God's Word still transforms lives. Each of you reminded me that discipleship is not a duty but a divine calling.

To the **young people** who inspired many of these chapters — your questions, your honesty, and your hunger for truth fueled my desire to write. May this book remind you that purpose still calls your name, and that you were truly born for more.

To my **family,** especially my daughters and grandchildren — thank you for your forgiveness, your laughter, and your love. You are my greatest earthly reward. You remind me daily that redemption is real, and that legacy begins at home.

To those who have read my previous works and continue to follow my writing journey — your faith and support keep me pressing forward. You remind me that words can heal, challenge, and change lives.

And to every reader holding this book:

Thank you for allowing me to speak into your life. If these pages have strengthened your faith, stirred your compassion, or renewed your hope, then the mission is complete.

All glory to God, who alone makes the seed grow.

About the Author

Restoring Faith, One Story at a Time.

Eld Joel Latimore Jr. is a U.S. Army veteran, author, and mentor whose life reflects the power of redemption through Jesus Christ. A native of Cleveland, Ohio, he is the founder of **Latimore Publishing,** a ministry committed to producing faith-based books that inspire spiritual growth and personal transformation.

Elder Latimore's writings are transparent, prophetic, and deeply practical—each one urging readers to walk by faith, not by assumption, but by the Spirit of God.

His growing body of work includes *Faith and Fire: Walking with the Holy Ghost*, *Not This Woman: Delilah's Spirit, the Strange Woman, and the Cost of Compromise*, *The Just Shall Live by Faith: Lessons from the Book of Romans*, and *Learning to Walk by Faith: Not by Assumption, But by the Spirit*.

Through writing and mentorship, Elder Latimore continues to reach hearts across generations, teaching that no one is too broken for God to heal or too far for His grace to find. His life and message remind us all that we were truly born for more.

www.ingramcontent.com/pod-product-compliance
Lightning Source LLC
Chambersburg PA
CBHW070614030426
42337CB00020B/3796